The Sunrise Scrolls

Lamine Pearlheart

OTHER BOOKS BY THE SAME AUTHOR

To Life from the Shadows

***

The Mayan Twins - At the Edge of Xibalba's Well

LAMINE PEARLHEART

PREFACE

A lot has happened, in my personal life and in the world, since I wrote the first part of " To Life from the Shadows".

I will not enumerate the woes the world witnessed since, but suffice it to say that I personally came out with a new perspective on things.

This new perspective can be perceived in the content of this new book, which I titled the "The Sunrise Scrolls", for indeed I felt a new awakening happening in me, and in the hope that it manifests in the world around me, I precede with this book.

I learned since that words alone, even if hoped for, provide no consolation to us unless we are ripe to hear them.

Also, that there are things in the world, under the weight of destiny and our natural progression, which need to be carried by each of us individually; grief and helplessness are some of them.

I observed that there is also some relief in the appreciative assessment of being, as one was and is, if timely weighed and perceived by the hopeless creature.

CONTENTS

To benevolence,

On Why Men Never Ask for Directions

He looked at the perfectly round moon soaring up in sky, he circled the setting sun with the corner of one of his primitive eyes, then he remembered the stars of the night before and how great they shone in the darkness, "Just like orbs of fire!" He told his wife before they entered their dwelling in the cave.

Now perched on a mountain, holding a spherical apple on his right hand, he looked at the curved horizon and said, "Yes, the Earth is indeed flat."

Nobility and Lineage

"Being related to the horse does not make the mule a noble mustang." – To those who believe that nobility is a matter of lineage

On Investment

An investment is deemed an investment only through its returns.

On Being Abandoned

You are not abandoned until you feel that you are!

The Source of Life

There is a beauty unlike anything described by the world religions; it has no name for it should not be called and no form for words are imperfect means to describe it; it is life and the source of life.

It knows no friends or foes for its clock beats for everyone; it gives and takes life and recomposes it again.

It smiles at everybody the same before it fades and reappears again.

I have known it in my consciousness all my life and I didn't recognize it for what it is, so much as it is undeservedly described by humankind, and I was using the mirrors of others to find it.

This entity is, I believe, what some mistakenly refer to as God.

The Bright Side

"Look at the bright side!" It was said many times and I must add, "That is the only thing that ever was!"

The Order of Things

Woman, you are what is beautiful in humankind; if only man was gifted with a heart to see!

Child, you are all that is sublime in humanity; if only it could stay in the form of angels!

Angels, you are what we wish to be; if only we listened to our souls instead of being lost in our hearts!

Dolphins, you are the infants we have lost, and your playful games on the surface and the deep remind us of our lost innocence as we became humans

Eagle, you will fly towards the heavens and perspectives to us inconsolable; your inspired jump is where our thoughts go when they will be undisturbed

God, we dreamed you as a response to our distresses and we have looked for you many times so that we can find you when we are lost in our assured delirium

Lady Earth, you always carry us despite our deceitful souls with no tomorrow; I console you

Age, you offer us advice, but we never from ourselves learn

Sun, bountiful, of you I confirm a reawakening

Immeasurable cosmos, towards you my eyes do rise and sets the curb of my pride

Being in me who says all this; I see you.

On Living

A great mind said once that "It is of humanity as it is of all other elements floating in awe" and a greater mind said...well it said nothing for it lived.

On the Human Situation

We are programmed to live forever and designed to die in a brief time

To be reassembled, but never to be broken apart

To get closer to the light, but in darkness to depart

The wisdom of humankind is to linger, but never to survive

We are being light glimmering in the eternal silence of the hive

Hoping to be able to carry on hoping in the face of the crude anonymous mind

When Angels Cease to Be

He looked at the baby and said, "Cute angel, he becomes human when he starts to believe that he is an angel."

The Weight of Evil

Before evil, all action that is unnecessary and unwarranted, tries to hurt and burden other people it needs to carry injury in itself.

On Humanity's Bewilderment

Prisoners of the sunlight marveling at the end of the day.

On the Necessity of Self-control

Everyone has a government in oneself and it needs to be watched for it is as unreliable as the ones ruling the earth.

Its plans are hidden from view for it is intimate and its constitution has only one clause; self-defence.

It is clearly one of the most covert regimes for its existence is rarely questioned or remembered. It is self-appointed and rules through misconceptions and fear. Its populace, the great values inserted through parental education and social interactions, are left in the darkness as to its functioning mechanism.

This regime needs to be constantly checked and corrected lest it corrupts the existence of its bearer.

The Stupid vs. the Criminally Insane

One thing the stupid and the criminally insane share in common is their disdain of the past and the fear of karma; the first due to the lack of good memory and the second for fear to be on the stand for the crimes committed.

On Karma

Karma does exist, not in the afterlife, but in this life and is mathematically linear, just like the number line; once one starts on the negative minus side of the scale, one continues to infinity in the same direction and so is the progression from the positive side.

Thus, at one point we all start from zero, but evil is blind and it never sees this progression even though it is obvious to the lightly discerning eye; it moves through the darkness heedlessly in an undisclosed progression, obvious to all, but to itself.

On Tolerating the Infamous

At the peril of letting yourself be surrounded by mosquitoes, you take the risk of being bitten.

On Tyrants

After conquering many lands and destroying many lives, the tyrant was swiftly disappointed for he recognized that there was one thing he could not rule and that was his self for he was consumed by his cruelty and a slave to his urges.

After all tyranny has to live with its despicable self; if it only could see the source of its unsatisfying madness!

On Hell on Earth

The hell the criminally disturbed raise is but a reflection of the one that is inside her or him.

Life Expectancy of Evil

Evil lives a lifetime, but goodness, all that is positive and done for no expected gain during this life or any presumed afterlife, lives.

On Revelation

"Revelation is what was hidden to someone and is suddenly revealed and which would otherwise still be hidden." It was said.

As far as the human religious experience is concerned, God is always revealed; this seems to be in agreement with all of the major world religions.

This experience, as reported, has been the lot of humanity for centuries and each and all of the religions are but documentation and interpretations of it.

Beyond this, there is the sad fact that they all claim to be the only true revelation.

On Giving with Ulterior Motives

The assistant gravedigger may carry the remains of the falling king, but it will never be his head upon which the crown will be wrought.

On Vagueness

Vagueness is the kingdom of the devil and it is as such on purpose.

Evil's Odour

"Thus, it was ordained for evil to have a particular stench repulsive to most and unbeknownst to its bearer."

The Fear of Death

You spend most of life afraid of death and when it comes you are thinking but of life; the opposite would perhaps be a better strategy.

About Evil

There is profiteering, capitalism, communism, and there is evil; it is the harvest of every clueless mind which does every deed for no monetary gain or purposeful goal. It is consumed by a repulsive force rejecting every one and itself.

When Death Cometh

When death comes, I will not be here for I will be dead.

On Misconceptions

"Believe me: you can go to underworld and have a great time as long as you have no misconceptions." – Heard it from the mouth of Hades.

On Zoos

A prison for animals who committed no crimes is what a zoo is.

On Evil's Predominance

Evil wants you to see evil everywhere, hence the "don't trust anyone" voice. How could that be if you're also anyone? Are you that arrogant to think that there is no one as honest as you? Or is it the dishonesty in you speaking loudly?

On Banks

Honesty becoming a corporation; that is what a bank is supposed to be.

Tyranny's Ethics

"If I could I would!" is the maxim of tyrants.

On Fear and Thought

The thought that is billed at the price of fear and flattery is as inconsolable as that which is paid for at the price of gold.

On Modern Slavery

Modern slavery, your heart understood it a while back my friend; it is but your brain which continues to deny it.

Your workplace is your home, and your home is but the registration and training centre for the new and future workers; your children.

On Religion and Grief

It is during grief and dire situations that faith is supposed to shine, rewarding the knowing mind through hope and fortitude, and that is unfortunately the precise moment when many believers choose to close their eyes.

As I See It

I like the sunrise and the moon

I need oxygen, water, and nourishments for my bones

I don't love my treasures; I use them to buy things and waste less time

I hope for the best knowing that I was not made to forever last

I see my end not as a new beginning, but as an accomplishment

I see evil and ask: is it senseless because it does not know that it is unnecessary or is it both?

When Sense is Incensed

After shooting everyone else and realizing that there was no one left to shoot, the sensible maniac shot himself on the foot.

"After all," he concluded, "This was in order."

On Freedom

Free your mind before you free your soul!

About Thinking

Thinking could be a form of recreation when done in style.

On the Weight of Belief

"While her fears are not factual, and the monster she fears do not exist, yet her emotions of fear are real.

Likewise, you may not believe that God exists, yet the belief in the Creator is, for the believer, as real as you and I and it has an impact on our world."

On Life After Death

"Are you afraid of death?"
"I am of the end of life. The afterlife does not scare me for this is where babies come from!"

On the Certainty of Death

"Well, you seem to be surprised that someone would want to kill you? In a world where lobsters are cooked alive, you, Mr. Jones looking at death, seem to be surprised!"

On the Origins of People and Things

"Being parented to the horse does not make the mule a noble steed!"

"But it sure points to the horse's roots and adds grace to his hereto humble achievements"

On Evolution

Degradation is also one of the traits of evolution.

On the Need to Extend One's Horizon

It is better to die with many wise persons than to die alone ignorant of the world.

On the Choice Between Terror and Tyranny

Yes, we are replacing the monster by a tyrant.

Some Sure Things

As sure as every citizen to his state is an enemy

As sure as the day hides the night

As sure as the night is but a daybreak in disguise

As certain and pending as an assault in a battlefield

Humanity of freedom is deluded and of itself mindless

Simple Rules

How not to die of poison?
Stop drinking it

How to stop terror?
Stop finance it

How to stop dying?
Stop living

How to become rich?
Pretend to be poor

How to stop them from warring?
Show them how much they are paying for it

How to learn something?
By admitting that you know nothing

How to become human?
By knowing that you are not

How to live forever?
By asking yourself if you deserved to be

How not to be alone?
Are you tired of your own company?

How to perceive angels?
By knowing that they too cannot see us

How to live life to the fullest?
By knowing that there is no such thing

On Humanity and God

"In the matter of God and our kind it is always everyone for oneself; it is an account that each one has to settle for oneself. Why religions, places of worship and congregations? I wonder." - *Words that a preacher had the indiscretion to say out loud*

On Devine History

God has always been an individual experienced conclusion; it is just that humankind presupposes to find the Creator revealed in a book or a tablet, even though those who were supposedly inspired to write them, we are told, never relied on any book, lived a solitary life, and shunned every congregation.

Why Family Is a Two-Way Street

"I am trying to win a sister and you are trying to lose a brother." Said a helpful youth to his sister.

On the Flexibility with the Villains and Bad Employees

The largesse with the rats brings but bigger holes in your net!

On Shooting Yourself on the Foot

Your nightmares need only you to unfold.

On Evil

Evil exists, I have seen it, it is a deed, and lucky for us it is not divine.

On Karma - *Addendum*

I have talked about how karma is mathematical and linear, how it has nothing to do with reincarnation but a state of affairs in this world, functioning like the number line in mathematics; symbolized with two directions "Plus and Minus", "0" being the dividing point, ad infinitum continuing forever in each direction.

Also, that once you have engaged in a negative action in life you make a step towards the negative side. Some actions may put you miles away into the negative side and are very hard to come back from, due to the heinousness of the action, to the positive point.

The fact of being grateful in your moments of grief and sadness, by remembering that you were better off than many in this world, tends to drop you from the negative side to the positive side.

This would help you better cope with things, even if it puts you at the "0" or "+1" positive points of the equation, as you would still be better off in facing the world for you gain a momentum of positive energy.

I repeat, "Being grateful is a good state of mind."

Just a Conversation

"I don't believe in God; I am a scientist!" Said a distinguished person.

"Yet, you believe that money is liquid and that it evaporates!" Said to him a less complex mind.

On Being Accepting of Others Way of Life

"Our senses to be offended!" is the fateful verdict and price set to be paid for being of an evolutionary nature.

Our State of Affairs in Eternity

You don't own, you only borrow, occupy time and space

You are neither rich nor poor for it is all a matter of seconds and perspectives

What was given to you must, before the end, be returned

What you envied for so long will fade

Under the weight of eternity, you are but a shade, a ghost, wrapped up in flesh and bones, finding its way home to the state of before birth.

The History of Slavery Continues

"You are tied up to an office desk like you were tied up to a pole! Yet, you committed no offence against your masters."

Why You Should Ignore the Delusional

Madness craves attention.

On the Unexpected

No problem is a surprise if you pay attention for you cannot see the ocean unless you see the waves.

The Challenge that Honest People Have in Front of Dishonesty

I have observed that dishonest people find it hard to believe honest people. Is it possible that they don't believe that honest people really do exist?

The Implied Last Words of Jesus on the Cross

When he was being crucified, on his last nanoseconds of life, nailed to the cross, Jesus shuddered in an endless awful pain which echoed through time and space.

He saw the round earth for the last time as his eyes were flung into space and back, seeing the earth for what it is, he said to humankind, though he could barely be heard, "Fools they put me upright, they don't see that they are upside down as the earth is hurled into space; I am the only one on this rock standing up! Be a lie!"

And so, it still is accursed, two thousand years after that, they are doomed to remember the date, but no to see the thing or be aware of what it is.

On the Merits of Hell and Paradise

An eternity in paradise or in hell seems to me to be disproportionate sentences in relation to actions performed during a short lifetime.

One might think that a happy or miserable subsequent life, of equal time, on earth, in proportion to the good or bad deeds committed, would be in good and due form.

This leads one to conclude that these eternal sentences are desired by either extremely vengeful or desperate creatures.

This seems to be the recurring position of humanity.

On the Respect of Other People's Beliefs

A book is as sacred as long as the people who hold it to be.

What You Don't See

Piercing and wiser is the light

Learn to talk to the rivers and speak to the seas

Be respectful of the oceans and salute the mountains

Humility a sharp inclination you must climb

Keep away from Xibalba and its vain lords

Fear is a thankless goddess even to the ingrates

Wars are the harvest of people with no souls; thieves of life and worshipers of Moloch, the seeker of ownerships, in disguise

Naked is the truth, no subterfuge required to make it shine, it speaks to everyone and none

Seek the arrows of compassion

Find your way through the maze

Love the creeping shadows of the light
Be the maker of good in the night

Soon enough you will disappear; ask what is of you, you wish to be left!

Learn to walk away from life before of you it does; be not the leech of things, but the maker of the useful ones

Hide not in disguise, and if you must, disappear into the light and in the goodness of all that is right

Fade in the oblivion of the spark,
The knowledge of the flame,
The warmth of the fire in the dreaded pale night,
The comfort of the transitory way to the upcoming avalanche of the glorious day

Remember that recycling was first invented by nature and you are but a fading reshaped line

Seek not eternity for the prerogatives of the source of life are not yours to decide

Answer for your deeds and be of the patience of the good seeds

Rise slowly like the sun and try to fade in likewise exquisite light

Arm yourself with the courage of the infant joyfully facing the unfavourable severe odds of life

See the strife, but live beyond its mind-numbing ridiculous cavernous grind

Find a way out!

Rise up and rise again!

On Tourism and Renewal

Every city, for its own sake, needs tourists for they are mostly excited to be in it and bring a regenerative energy flow through their contagious excitement; if you are feeling low go where they hang out and get some rebirth in this life.

On Truth and Reconciliation with Oneself

I have this mirror that makes me look thin and fit and every time I look at it, it plays to my vanity; I go to see her when I feel bloated and not particularly in good health, and it tells me that I have the body of a Greek god.

What it doesn't know is that I have that other mirror that tells me the opposite.

Now, I have a third and fourth mirror which I trust more, they show me no reflections of me, but are the source of my visions and bring me down from the clouds to a soberer look; these are my eyes.

On the "H" of the "P"

At the heart of every human problem faced, there is a human heart; you only have to remember this to solve it.

On Being Owned by Things

"You think that you own the earth just because you have a piece of paper that says so. Can you own the air? Can you take it with you when you die? All you have is but a temporal right of occupation and the right to transfer it to others.

As you have already observed nothing in life last forever."

When Prayers Are Blasphemy

"You are one of those people who believe that they can tell God what to do through prayers!"

The Compass of the Honest

If you are lost and not sure which way to go, remember that the best way to go is always the one that is right.

God and Feudalism

You call God, "Lord" and attribute to the Divine the traits of your vain and cruel feudal lords, and you still refer to the Creator as "he" and "him" as most of them were indeed males.

Thus, you portray the Creator as a vengeful, vindictive overlord, sadistically burning his serfs and disobedient subjects in eternal fires.

You don't see how the sun shines on all alike with no distinction or discrimination.

Satan's Utopia

"What is Satan's lifetime goal?"

"Do you mean the moral story behind the tale of this character?"

"Well, he is shit out of luck knowing his endeavors will fail; he will not be able to defeat the Almighty, so what is his angle?"

"I think he has none; he probably believes himself to be righteous, and like any delusional being he thinks that he will somehow make it through."

Our Perception of People

I was so excited to get into the water that I don't remember how I made it from the beach tent to the shore; the sun blinding rays didn't help either.

The first thing I saw was the damn incoherent waves; cold and unpredictable.

I cursed my luck and walked back to the beach disappointed, deciding that it was not worth the risk, then I suddenly looked back and saw the beautiful ocean looking back at me.

From there, I concluded that we must not confuse the difficulties we may have with a person or an issue with their overall perception.

The Desire to Live Eternally

The hope of living eternally is for me but the sneaky vow of humankind to be on the same level as the Creator.

I find this objectionable for I believe that we are soliciting a divine right which is not ours.

On Hell

There's a hell, it is called "Pretending to be someone else."

On Religion's Claims

"One of the mistake people make is equating God with organized religion, which, with its distorted view, proclaim itself as the divine order and its sole form of communication." – *From a conversation I had with Thomas Paine*

On Communication

"Nothing is understood that is not explained." - *A very simple rule that seems to be ignored by many.*

On Good Deeds with Bad Manners

You don't serve caviar with a punch to the face. Likewise, don't expect people to be grateful if your manners are failing.

On Mediocrity

Mediocrity is always predictable, mediocre people always rise up to sink lower, excellence and brilliance are not.

On the Value of Trust

Trust is earned and never given, those who give it freely are fools.

The Way I see it

My vengeance on the vile, the mediocre and their companions is the sunset followed by the sunrise

My justice on the unfair and the uncouth is the almighty time

My recourse against the perfidious and sickly in volition is the summer breeze followed by the recurring awaiting tide of the oceans

The depth of darkness cannot stand up to the presence of and lightness of air

My joy is the birth of a child and the like echoing sounds of dolphins; the playfulness of innocence

To the shadows of uncertainty, I offer the blinding rays of great potential

To the punishment of the bully his own deformed measure,

The tears of the clown and the memory of himself or herself to the rest of us

The wisdom of the insignificance of death when you have nothing to live for

The futility of power, treasures, and fame when you have so little time

To ignorance I throw no fist, no stone, no matter of great destruction

I flow like a river and reflect back my clarity to the dull eyes of the incredulous minds

Like an undying phoenix, I form my own self and in the air, I rise, subtle, but still fly with the same strides

I come to life every morning from a nightly death certain of my tomorrow

Every day I see,

To the darkness of the night the streaming light of the moon and the stars

To the apparent abyss of the universe the soothing colours of the quasars

To our incomprehension of the unbalanced the humanity of its members

These Are

These are before the goodbyes

The things I know, the ones I wish I didn't know yet

The tolling bell with my fading name on it

The horizon of tomorrow I will not see

The sunrise in all its glory reflected on my still breathing eyes; all that was and still could be, and all that still is

I witnessed the ignominy of my self, yet the beautiful spark that gave me life my good intent tempered and the wild in me tamed

Grateful life endured

Favored for being and not instead

I thought, I never left anything to chance, my steps firm on a long well laid plan I never knew when I set. My resolve covered my ignorance, and my ignorance my lack of tact

We do not die, we become unborn, for to die we need not be born

The Meaning of Life

"The ultimate meaning of life is life itself. How could it be any other way?"

The Invisible Brush

The girl was dancing, but there was no music, she held on to the hand of her mother with her left hand and twisted her tiny body in the air as she walked along with her parents.

The poet saw in this the work of the muse and wrote a song,

The spiritual, the hand of God and a reiteration of an early program,

The scientists, an instinctive gesture and a willed emotional motion,

The religious, well he did not see anything for he kept his senses locked up in a single book that humans created and forgot about the divine,

The brush artist saw an occasion for a painting in his workshop to hang, a reminder of his limits and of things he willingly cannot understand;

The mystery of the essence of the world not needing to be analysed,

The joy to be found and fading under the inquisitive eyes

The angels, they thanked their maker and saw themselves in the child, they recognized the wealth of humankind; a birth and a rebirth again.

On National Cultures

"The so-called culture of nations are as real as individuality and free spirits in herds; finding it is the way of the dodo. I do rather seek culture in the ambient individual being."

Why Justification Has Nothing to Do with It

"Behind every vile crime there is a sense of self-righteousness."

On Stereotypes

In the world of the particular, the devil is in the details, in that of propaganda he is in the generalization. They are called blanket statements for a reason; to dull the senses in preparation for sleep and your conscience to legitimize its entombment.

On Pride and Vanity

"Amongst the great desert sands, he was a prominent particle." - To be written on the tomb of my vanity

A Recollection

I lived through time immemorial because my fading memory says I did so

I saw humanity's sad fate; a brave faceless light in the darkness seeking that which is as brilliant

A spark of courage, amongst the perilous assaulting waves, floating on the last sinking wave

On Impressing People

"Trust me I don't want to be me; I have met me and I was not impressed to say the least."

What Does the Sun Do?

"Why do you do it everyday? You have nothing to gain from it?" Asked the moon.

"Because it is great idea becoming reality." The sun responded.

On Our Elected Official

"He is so unreal that I can almost see the puppeteer's strings."

On Knowledge

It is better to have little knowledge that takes you distances than have a lot of knowledge that keeps you nowhere, and worst no knowledge at all.

An All-New Perception

The more extraordinary I felt my circumstances to be the more unsatisfyingly ordinary my life seemed to appear.

On What You Are

You are but a living record of yourself.

On Why Owls Don't Speak

A wise person says well what he or she thinks, but is wary of himself or herself and what he or she says.

Being in Love

Love makes you uncertain about things and it makes you feel unfit. Is she the cause or is she the reason?

On Why You Have Not Yet Met Your Ideal Mate

Sometimes the question, when it comes to love, is not if one is capable of loving, but if one is ready to.

The Tricky Thing About Stereotypes

A stereotype is based on an observation of something that is real, but the stereotype itself is not.

A Potential Solution to Unfulfilled Electoral Promises

There are people to whom one needs to say what to do, and others to whom one must leave additional instructions on what not to do.

On Mass Consumption

"The poorer you are, the more crap you shall have." - *This is the commandment of our modern mass consumption society.*

On the State of the Future

The future is but trust and hope

On Everlasting Love

We love those we believe are better than us, and we better make sure that the attraction is not for a single trait; lasting love requires a mutual willingness to sacrifice for one another.

Camaraderie, a tiny portion of love, will take you only so far; love is another being altogether.

On the Digital World

"We did a full contour from memory to solid paper and now to memory again. We learned since ancient times how treacherous memories are and we pledged a covenant on paper to protect ourselves, and then when we thought we tamed the unyielding beast, it managed to break the gates of time, preserving itself in the recesses of our conscience, it reveals itself in the virtuosity of zeros and ones."

On Wasted Time

"We think that we are important because we are part of something bigger than us, so we talk about world affairs of which we evidently have no say, thus carrying a burden that is not ours, and we forget to dedicate time to the most important thing; the "self" that is in each one of us." - *On investing, with no tangible return, the little time we have on listening to politicians and presstitutes.*

The Persistence of Love

Love is a flower that is always given

Can you keep it blooming in the face of the tides?

Some put it in a vase for the rest of the day

Artful masters keep holding on to the seeds

The storms may flicker the light

The waves may inundate the intrepid heart

Beware of the doubtful deeds

Nothing lasts forever and for a lifetime you can hold on eternally

I imagine the manners; a genuine spirit of the truth is never shy

The sunrise is never of the moon in envy of the twilight

Diamonds are never challenged by the preposterous shining golden lights

On the Dangers of Little Knowledge

"Not because we don't understand why and how something works that it necessarily means that it is absurd; life is one of those things."

Love

"Love is a ship that comes with great style cruising in the harbour and making impressive waves." Said a sailor looking at incoming ships.

"It is an earthquake giving no warning and leaving only the wreckages of your former self." Said a broken heart.

Older friends say, "It is an ageless grip, it takes what it marks and its victims are not always happy with the sip; there is no guarantee for the take."

"No, it is a hurricane and I welcome the opportunity for a change." Said a daredevil.

The wizards and fools are not immune for all rush headlong towards the accidents they equally call a bliss

I know that it moves through time like a mirage and breathes its nectar to the unsuspecting host, rising through the fall and disastrous encounters, to make a picture of a gorgeous smile, a loving touch, and an awakening of the dormant anchored mist

You find yourself in front the promise and extend your hand to take a grip

The beautiful ghost owns your thoughts and is sailing through your soul infusing you with potentials

For the first time, the mirrors and shadows are not lying

For the first time, the angels and sirens are one and the same

For the first time and at last you are yourself before you become joined

Canada

At first, as I met her, l thought she was lost until she said, "Of the rest of world, I am not afraid,

Some of those who inspired me where not from here

People come to me not to become, but to be

I like them the way they are, they add colour to my blue sea

I am the friend of the restless, see them as brighter as they can be

See them as they see me

Restful in my arms, yet invisible is my nurturing light
They smile now, nothing more precious to a mother than a happy child who is polite

I am the star you want to see, the hope you want to set free

Mine is the Commonwealth of the world to be"

Before she walked away, she flipped a toonie into my direction and said, "Not much, but remember to give back."

Those who know her are smitten by her grace
Those who don't know her seek her embrace

It is said that she watches over the northern abode of the gods, the gates of which, when she blushes, are marked by northern lights

A rising majestic colourful totem of peace signals her tempered western profile

It is her birthday tomorrow and I ask, "What do you give a beautiful lady who has everything?"

Lady Canada says, "just a genuine smile."

The Power of Goodness

In goodness evil is obliterated.

On Love and War

"All is fair in love and war." Is said by people who know nothing about love nor war, and worst have no intention of loving or warring.

On Living

"It is a beautiful life, live you fools! What are you waiting for?" Says the sun every day before dying.

On Helping Others

You can teach people to fly, you may give them wings, but if they are not willing to soar, your efforts would be just dead weight for them and for you.

On the Ingrates and Good Will

"Here I am thinking that I am helping while you were thinking that I was serving." Said good will to purpose.

On Vanity

Your eyes told me more than your voice ever could

I have watched the moon fall with lesser warp

I have seen the sun shimmer with lesser curves

I remember a rose singing to mindless birds

People shining looking at diamonds and in silence were telling themselves, "What a great reflection we make!"

I saw the proud bison driven over a cliff by a lesser opponent

Tamed horses running wild

I saw your eyes and now I understand why

You can try mending shattered glass

You cannot mend broken eyes for what they see is not outside

You can tell them lies and truths they don't understand

You cannot hide what is inside bound for the way out

You can coax time and give him fleeting endless signs, but he knows that permanence is his, the tool to the unraveling of the pride of our kind

The reason for our continuous demise

On Corporate Service

It is where dreams come to die

It is where perversion has a soul

It is a vessel whose lullaby desensitizes

When You Must Stop Talking

With some people, continuing to argue is like pursuing a butterfly; just let it go and it will come your way.

On Why I Seldom Frown

They are laughing with me, at me, the importance is that they are laughing.

My Remains

Part of me in the light of the morning star

Part of me in the air I breath and the last one on this rock, in the this form I will air

I am the passing corpse becoming a precious thought

The hungry plant feeding on invisible light

I am the child of war meeting the infant of hope shortly playing ball

I am the one distinct individual in the "All!"

The promise of the sun coming back tomorrow

I am the grief chasing the futile sorrow

I am birth vanquishing death

The seagulls finding the shore

I am time obliterated by sound

The unexpected fortune knocking on your door

I am the flower daring to bloom on solid ground

I am the unexplained beating heart

I am the human potential to the insignificance of fear

I am the useless yet sought after colourful rainbow

I am with the one who with his last breath said, "I may break but will not bow"

I am the life-giving seed to the presumptuous weed

I am the one who sinks low to find pearls of rainbow

I am positive waves of relief chasing grief

The long light of day chasing the nightmarish night

The horizon to the aircraft carrier

The sunrise to the gates of sunset

I am myself to this ephemeral body

The continuation of all that is good beyond I

All that is and to be

On Your Day of Grief

You were privileged for life lent you a precious gift; it gave before it took back.

It showered you for a lifetime with joy, but in one day, just on that day, it reminded you that you were chosen for the gift became a precious thought the day your loved one passed on.

Gratitude should be your course now and in that there is immense relief.

Life is still gifting you and if you just look forward and around, you should see other gifts by your side.

Look.

Choices

Between pride and doing the right thing, do the right thing. Don't let negative perception ever stop you from doing what is inherently good.

On Being Mean

The crap you throw at people you still must carry it to able to do so.

Looking back on moments of self-definition

Sometimes, even if it seems so, you are not lost, but finding yourself.

On Priding Yourself for Being Part of a Select Group

Importance is a matter of circles and so are zeros.

Sorry as a State of Mind

Apologies if not meant and not followed up with concrete actions are like adding oil to a low and receding fire; you think you are just keeping it alive, but you may ignite it further sparking unexpected wildfires.

On the Need of Enemies

Your enemies add urgency to your endeavors, but do nothing to inspire them if your mind is in order and set in its course. In brief, you don't need them to define you.

The Secret of Becoming Rich

You want the secret of making gold so that you can exchange it for money. You see I understand the absurdity of your logic.

Grief's Endurance

Do you really recover from the passing of a loved one?

The pain may recede, but the gravity of the thought is always stronger; to expect less is an indication of how we truly feel about that person.

On Putting Longer Hours at Work

"You work so hard as if you are running from something or someone. You don't seem eager to go home."

To the Edge

I will walk you to the gates of hell, because this is where we are heading you and I, I will see you through, and walk out to the other side.

Pushed to the limit

You take someone to the gates of hell, you better be ready to get in.

What Communism and Capitalism Have in Common?

Both want the punching bag to love the boxer.

To the Lazy Buggers

No empires were built by beggars.

What You Value

"When my father died, do you know what he took with him?"

"What?"

"Nothing. The fact that you ask makes me wonder, and tells me that you still cling to things."

When You Get More than You Bargained For

You don't want to harvest the clouds; they bring the hurricanes and the floods.

The Power of Words

"When I am done with you, even the trash bin will not want you." Said a publicist to a boxer.

On Dogs and Fire Hydrants

Why do dogs hate fire hydrants? Because fire hydrants piss them off.

Questions Asking Themselves

"Who is the smartest person on earth? Who was the most intelligent person in the history of humankind? Who is the best-looking person in the world?" Are all questions asked by the dumb and responded to by the least intelligent; it has been noted that they are frequently one and the same.

The Root of Discontent

If you took the trouble to initially hear my voice, instead of ignoring me, you would not have had to endure the displeasure of hearing my screaming voice now.

Sympathy vs. Respect

"I would rather have your respect rather than your sympathy."

"Why?"

"I observed that respect last longer."

On the Academical Teaching of History

Modern history does but describe the past through dates and events, but never explains them.

The Secret About Prayers

"In every book, one hears the distinct voice of the writer; it is likewise in the creation for it echoes that of its Maker.

I have also observed that sometimes the Creator responds before you ask and if you understand this you will find the replies superbly waiting for you." - *I overheard two angels talking the other day.*

What It Takes

It takes more than beauty, it needs honesty

Sometimes it is about the right timing not the lack of will

It is needs more than readiness, it sometime requires both willing hearts and an aversion to cheat

The cloudless vision of a heart beat

The rhythm of a soft and loving voice

The clarity of a good choice

The wisdom of the sun meeting the horizon

The truth of the stars to that of the vision

The moon leaning, but fair

A walk away from the angry steps leading to the underworld, consciously heading back to the lightness of air

The importance of the little drops to the making of the sea

The complexity of the being in me

The simplicity of it all in an "I"

Seeing you and me

No vision, but certainty

No greed extending to the promise of eternity

Just the knowledge of this life, gratitude for being

The preciousness of it all and its brevity

The unknown face of decency meeting the sceptical

It is not about owning a stake in futility

All passes, nothing is taking with the dying air

Precious as good manners are good memories

The will to go on

The State of Gratitude

Gratitude is not a sentiment that someone tells you to be in, it is, I am afraid, a conclusion and a rebellious stage you have to reach on your own.

On Usefulness

"You serve no purpose, but to us you are useful." Says Capitalism to the proletariat.

On Disappointment

We are never disappointed with people we think little of, those who disappoint us are thus by definition of importance to us.

On Life After Death

You will not be resurrected, but recomposed you will be for certain.

A Vision

The angel perched his wings on the façade of the column

From above, he was looking at the world beneath

The birds in envy flew to the summits of the mountains

Men and women, with the exception of the children, look at him as if he were an emerging island

Angels do recognize each other in the darkness of light and in the noise of regained silence

Peaceful, a child approaches the angel, he asks that humanity be forgiven, "This world is much more modest that we thought it to be." Said he while pointing to an illusion

The day hides its waves of light

The eagles point their beaks to show the way

Shivers humanity in its ignorance, the winter draws nearer to the horizon

Prayers of tomorrow in a universal sense

Emerges an island in the depth of the sea embalmed by light

Run the swallows towards the sun

Anticipated is the ship, now in the horizon, carrying a promise from another world

With a single breath on its sails, the ship fades away

Seek the eyes a being awaited; the Creator emerging in glory

Clever are the jackals, from a distance they await the outcome of the event, seeking options to trade with the dupes

Do they think that this time they will be emerging?

Sees the poet the whole in the all; the planet without wings flying in space,

A smile of appreciation in the depth of the heart,

Rich by knowing, poorer when believing,

Could he find a finer muse?

Marching are the columns of children towards the gates of the sun

Only innocence sees the way

Wide open are the doors of the places of worship; spits pretension its last alms

"Daring to lock the Creator in one spot!" Exclaim the angels with echoes from up above

Sing the shells their last sea rhymes

Finally, in effervescence, revealed is benevolence to those who know it

An idea with no veil is drawn on the hearts of animals, except for the human adults

"Make your heart beat, if you have one, and rejoin the sun!" Says a voice

Devoid, humanity, with no innocence, unveils itself without a heart and thus with no heartbeats

"No heartbeats for the jackals in disguise." Observes an infant

Scream the crows, finally understood the sound of their shrill complaints, they point to the adult bipeds, now marching, no lines, only sad beings, preys to their own stubbornness

Cry the tears at the end of the path

The last sunset plunges up

Darkness engulfs the earth, except, where shines the heart of a child

A decree? A proposition? Or is it a promise?

Strange is the scene to an ephemeral creature,

Yet…

On Change

"An entry or an exit door is still a door; it is an opportunity to the wise and just a piece of hardware to the fool." - May the fool in me remember.

When Beauty is Redundant, Yet Still Appealing

"You don't need one you are already one." To a beautiful lady holding a flower.

On Knowing Ourselves

In order to know about others, we need to know ourselves, and we seem to know little about ourselves as so much of it is filled with the stuff of others.

Where I Come From

"Have you ever wondered about the clouds? They carry enough water to melt mountains, enough liquid to flood whole countries and continents.

The weight of their content makes the seas and oceans, yet they float on air are made of air.

As such is the lightness and splendour of my world. " - *Heard it from a Dolphin.*

On intellectual Conversations

Conversations that stir the mind are bound to stir the soul.

On Honesty

Honesty is never a state of being, it is always something you want to achieve. To state otherwise demonstrates the presence of an undercurrent of dishonesty. *On why I try to be honest*

On the Importance of Self-revulsion

You need to vomit yourself multiple times to get rid of the scum that reside in you, and

when you do try to muster the strength to see
the defects still in you.

The Source Code

She walks to the rhythm of the sound of her
footsteps

She tries to fall under the weight of her
weak tiny little legs as if made of glass

She is under the watchful vision of the
Divine whom she does not see

Like time she clearly measures the distances
ahead of her

Out of nowhere, her arms hold the air;
looking for the supportive hands of a loving
parent not invented to be there

The first human child, extends her arms, she
searches for her tomorrow and clamours for a
place in a world in full effervescence,

"Is she going to fall flat on her face?" The
jealous rats enquire of each other

"Is she going to soar up?" The eagles in the air alarmingly ask themselves

No one sees nor proclaim her nudity as indecent; humanity did not yet see itself more conscientious than its maker

She follows her destiny like a flower in bloom

She hardly breathes and her short breaths she holds like precious gold

She picks up a flower and extends it to the heavens with laughter as fresh as a source of water and dolphin like echoes filling up the fault lines of the heart

In spite of the rats, in spite of the eagles she always continues on her walk

Under the eyes of Benevolence, she receives but does not see that she does

The sun illuminates her, could that be a Divine smile?

On the Usefulness of Prayers

"I don't ask to receive or to be given for I was blessed without asking and sheltered before I could wonder how

I ask in order to be humbled lest I forget how I departed

If the Creator wills it then I shall receive it

If the Creator does not will it then I do not need it and I should not regret not having it

If I cry then I hope the tears would be of gratitude

Of the uncertainty of death, I dare not fear for my path will be lit and in the darkness, I shall see the brilliance of my benefactor and maker

In grief, I shall try to remember that the lifetime generous giver should not be mistrusted for taking back what was in right not to give."

"The above is my favourite prayer." Said an atheist.

On Making It Through

In life, you may not have the choice of action, but you always have a choice of reaction; react positive and your life will be less miserable and perhaps more abundant.

On Seeing the Obstacles for What They Are

You swim better if you lose the presumption of full control.

On Those Important to Us

The sun rising or setting is still the sun, the glory and beauty of its coming and leaving is not diminished by its beginning or end.

Creation

"I know there is this entity that created our world, beyond that all I see is human worshipping human or whatever human said." – *Repeat to each other the sacred books every time they see a human approaching them*

The End of the Battle between Good and Evil

Coming from a long and perfectly productive retreat, the Devil stood in front of his people proud and illuminated for he had reinvented himself and had brand new ideas to share with them.

The temple was filled with applause from every loge for his return was warmly expected.

The Devil suddenly said, in a loud yet sharp voice, "First, in addition to the usual wars and mayhem, we will put dead fish remnants in the chicken and beef feed, they may get Alzheimer and be mad, but that it is ok for it is a risk we are willing to take," he quickly looked at the audience and continued, "then we inject the animals with hormones and put them in cages."

He paused as if he remembered something, then added, "Some people complained about the cages? Well, we will let them be free range in bigger cages. How about that? Not good enough?"

He looked questioningly at the members and resumed, "Ok, we will let them graze outdoors on pesticide and GMO contaminated fields so that their DNA is altered."

He heard the start of a single applause, and interrupted it saying, "Wait I am not done yet. Once we slaughter them, we wash them with bleach, process them with carcinogenic chemicals, and send them to the supermarket for mothers and children to eat them; diabolical, right?"

As he finished his speech, the devil looked around to see the effects his Action Plan had on the audience.

Unfortunately for the devil he didn't know the reason behind the placid reception for he had been away for a long time.

A trembling voice, dressed in a black suit of the latest fashion, in whisper reached out to him and said, "Humankind has already done that."

Shaken and almost faltering to the ground, his face profusely sweating, he fell to his knees and in disbelief he looked up to the heavens for relief.

He croaked right then and there.

The devil was finally beaten by the sons and daughters of humankind.

A Recovery

I grieved for myself before the sunset

My morning not coming to me was not a bet

Looked at the heavens to seek what to find

Emptiness was the sound meeting my extended index and extenuating mind

Inside, but acceptance of my fate

The pain receding with every contemplated light

Like the brave bound and chained to the resolute hope

Emerging from the hollow attempts of my last breath, rose a strident silent voice

"Don't you dare give up!" Said the echoes

My morning light ripped the night

I walked like a frail old man; my body aching with every vibration of my hollow bones

My world on hold, the heavens passive, the shadows held back by an entity I could not define

It is then that I saw it written on my mind

Memory of an invisible helpful hand

Conscience unwrapping the maker of its last stand

Days walked by heavy like lead

Heartbeats drumming the nearing end

There was no vision, no signs

Just an entity dwelling in the best part that is in me

Energy flowed from whence there was none

Fire burned where water rained

Crystallized waves pierced the dark night

Light, piercing light unseen, touched the hollow being in me

I watched as the day vanquished the night

Hope superseded fear

Wisdom in all that I did not understand

Pompous futility crashed by eternity

Beauty; a consolation to the weary mind

Life, but life

And I am become life, extraordinary life

ABOUT THE AUTHOR

Lamine Pearlheart is an avid reader and, as far as he remembers, he always had a great appreciation for literature, history, philosophy, poetry, and enjoys long walks as a meditation form.

One of his chief interests is the understanding of the human experience in its multidimensional aspects as is apparent in his books.

He also has a passion for languages; he speaks English, French, German, Spanish and Portuguese.

The author is currently working on his first novel.